The Minutemen

by **Lucia Raatma**

Content Adviser: Richard J. Bell,
History Department,
Harvard University

Reading Adviser: Susan Kesselring, M.A.,
Literacy Educator,
Rosemount-Apple Valley-Eagan (Minnesota) School District

COMPASS POINT BOOKS
MINNEAPOLIS, MINNESOTA

Compass Point Books
3109 West 50th Street, #115
Minneapolis, MN 55410

Visit Compass Point Books on the Internet at *www.compasspointbooks.com*
or e-mail your request to *custserv@compasspointbooks.com*

On the cover: Minutemen fire at British soldiers during the Battle of Concord on April 19, 1775.

Photographs ©: Bettmann/Corbis, cover, 6, 8, 13, 16, 26, 28, 31, 33, 39; Prints Old & Rare, back cover (far left); Library of Congress, back cover; DVIC/NARA, 5 (top); North Wind Picture Archives, 5 (bottom), 15, 23, 30, 35; James L. Amos/Corbis, 7; Stock Montage/Getty Images, 9; Stock Montage, 10, 22, 34; Yale Center for British Art, Paul Mellone Collection/The Bridgeman Art Library, 11; Corbis, 17; Louis S. Glanzman, 18; James P. Rowan, 21 (all), 27, 40; William L. Clements Library, University of Michigan, 24; National Park Service, artist John Rush, photographer Michael Tropea, Chicago, 36–37.

Creative Director: Terri Foley
Managing Editor: Catherine Neitge
Editor: Nadia Higgins
Photo Researcher: Svetlana Zhurkina
Designer/Page production: Bradfordesign, Inc./Les Tranby
Cartographer: XNR Productions, Inc.
Educational Consultant: Diane Smolinski

Library of Congress Cataloging-in-Publication Data
Raatma, Lucia.
  The minutemen / by Lucia Raatma.
      p. cm. — (We the people)
  Includes bibliographical references and index.
  Audience: Grades 4–6.
  ISBN 0-7565-0842-8 (hardcover)
  1. Minutemen (Militia)—Juvenile literature. 2. United States—History—Revolution, 1775–1783—Juvenile literature. 3. Minutemen (Militia)—Massachusetts—Juvenile literature. 4. Lexington, Battle of, Lexington, Mass., 1775—Juvenile literature. 5. Concord, Battle of, Concord, Mass., 1775—Juvenile literature. 6. Massachusetts—History—Revolution, 1775–1783—Juvenile literature. I. Title. II. We the people (Series) (Compass Point Books)
  E255.R23 2004
  973.3'4—dc22   2004016307

TABLE OF CONTENTS

READY IN A MINUTE!

In the early 1700s, the United States was not yet a nation. Instead, the 13 American colonies were controlled by the government of Great Britain. For this reason, the colonies didn't have their own regular army. They relied on a militia of part-time soldiers.

The 13 American colonies

A Minuteman is called to service while plowing his field.

Some of the most highly trained and experienced soldiers volunteered for special service within the militia. These special soldiers were called Minutemen because they were expected to be ready in a moment's notice. When the call came up for their services, they would leave their homes, their

A Minuteman receives a blessing as he goes to battle.

5

Minutemen had no uniforms. They supplied their own clothes and weapons.

farms, or their businesses right away.

Minutemen could be as young as 16 or as old as 60, though most were 25 or younger. Dressed in their ordinary work clothes and carrying muskets they had bought with their own money, they would report for training.

These men often trained for four hours at a time, usually twice a week, although this training varied from town to town. In bad weather, some Minutemen even trained in their leaders' kitchens! They practiced marksmanship, which is shooting weapons at a target. They also learned about strategy and the best way to fight the enemy.

6

Actors practice firing muskets similar to those used by the Minutemen. By today's standards, the weapons didn't shoot far and had very poor aim.

Previously, some of these Minutemen had fought in conflicts with American Indians. Since the colonists were living on land that the Indians once had to themselves, there were a number of battles between the two groups. However, the Minutemen really become well known during another conflict—the American Revolutionary War against Great Britain.

7

SETTING THE STAGE FOR WAR

For many years, the colonies didn't mind being ruled by Great Britain. The Americans went about their daily lives as farmers and merchants. They didn't worry too much about British lawmakers in Parliament or their king, George III.

King George III of England

Then in the 1760s and 1770s, things began to change. Great Britain was in debt because of a long, expensive war with France. So Parliament wanted to earn more money for its government. Lawmakers there decided to charge a tax on some items sold in the colonies. These items included newspapers, tea, and sugar. The colonists did not like having to pay these taxes. They felt they should not have to help support the British because they had no voice in that government.

8

Before long, a number of the colonists, known in the colonies as patriots, began to protest. They met in groups and talked about ways to deal with the British. Sometimes the colonists' frustration with the British got out of hand.

In March 1770, a group of patriots took aim at the British troops in their city. They threw sticks, rocks, and snowballs at the soldiers. They dared the troops to fight back. Finally, the British soldiers did fight back, firing their weapons and killing five colonists. This incident came to be called the Boston Massacre.

About three years later, in December 1773,

During the Boston Massacre of 1770, British soldiers fired at American colonists.

9

Disguised as Indians, colonists destroy boxes of British tea.
This event would come to be known as the Boston Tea Party.

the patriots protested British rule again. One night a group of men, dressed as American Indians, crept onto British ships in Boston Harbor. Then they dumped boxes and boxes of British tea into the water. This act, later known as the Boston Tea Party, was the colonists' way of making sure no one ever paid taxes on that tea.

These events made King George III very angry. He got Parliament to pass tougher laws against the colonists and sent more troops to Boston. Among those to arrive was General Thomas Gage, who then became the military governor of the Massachusetts colony. Gage was also furious about the colonists' actions and took

British General Thomas Gage enforced the British king's unpopular laws in Massachusetts.

11

pride in keeping order and making sure Parliament's laws were obeyed. Yet the more the British tried to control the American colonists, the more daring the Americans became.

General Gage soon realized that allowing the colonists to have weapons was a major threat to the British. He and the king decided to seize the supplies of gunpowder, muskets, and cannons that the colonists were gathering. One such supply was located in Concord, Massachusetts, about 19 miles (31 kilometers) from Boston. When patriot spies heard that General Gage was planning to take these weapons, they spread the news, and patriot leaders soon came up with a plan. The Minutemen would play a key role in that plan.

12

ANSWERING THE CALL

The Minutemen were brave and clever, but they were also just ordinary citizens. Most of the time, they tended shops or worked on farms. They were struggling to make a living, and most did not have a lot of money. They could not afford all the new taxes, and they realized that they would have to stand up to the British.

On the night of April 18, 1775, the Minutemen got their chance. This was the night of Paul Revere's famous ride through the Massachusetts countryside. Revere was a well-known silversmith who lived in Boston. He and

Paul Revere warned the Minutemen that British troops were on the march.

William Dawes were sent by Dr. Joseph Warren, a patriot leader, to Lexington, a town near Concord. The two men were to warn patriot leaders that British soldiers were on their way.

Along the way, Revere rode his horse from house to house. He woke up Minutemen and told them of the British advance. Over the years, the story that Revere yelled "The British are coming! The British are coming!" has become a legend. However, it is probably more accurate that he yelled, "The Regulars are coming!" *Regulars* was another name for the British troops. No matter what he yelled, he made lots of noise and wasted no time telling the Minutemen that they were needed.

The soldiers jumped out of bed, got dressed, and prepared to protect their weapons supply in Concord. No doubt, they were a bit scared as they left their homes. They had no idea what lay before them or what the day would hold. Some of the Minutemen were older and had military experience. Others, however—especially those who were

News of the approach of British troops spread quickly through the night.

only 16 or 17 years old—must have wondered what they were getting into.

One leader of the Minutemen was Captain John Parker, and he was among the men awakened that April night. Parker was born in Lexington and made a living as a farmer and a mechanic of farming equipment. He had fought in the French and Indian War (1754–1763), so he had some experience as a soldier. He gathered about 70 Minutemen to face the British at Lexington Green, the town's village square.

A Minuteman leaves his family to face the British.

The first battle of the Revolutionary War was fought on Lexington Green.

Parker didn't know how many British troops were on their way. He didn't know what they would do. Would they march on by? Would they fire? He did know, however, that he was about to face units of the most powerful army in the world. Parker wanted to make a stand against the approaching army. He wanted to uphold

17

the town's honor, but he realized that he would have to be careful. He did not block the road to Concord, which would have prevented the British from marching through town. He also told his men not to fire unless the British fired first.

Captain John Parker and his men waited hours for the British to arrive at Lexington Green.

THE BATTLE OF LEXINGTON

About 700 British soldiers were marching from Boston toward Concord under the command of Lieutenant Colonel Francis Smith. These soldiers soon realized their movements were no longer a surprise to the colonists. It was not yet dawn on April 19, 1775, but lights were on in homes, and the colonists were awake. Smith feared trouble, and he sent a message back to General Gage in Boston asking for more soldiers.

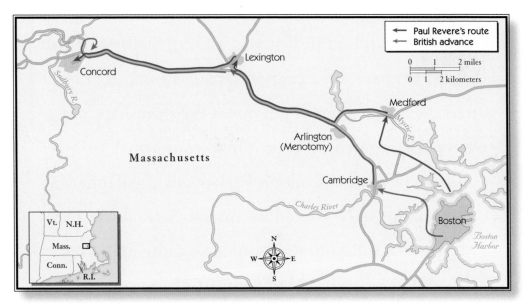

This map shows the route Paul Revere took on the night of April 18, 1775. It also shows British movements on April 19.

As the British marched on, Captain Parker and his Minutemen were watching and waiting. They listened for the sounds of drums and footsteps. When the British finally arrived at Lexington Green, they must have been a frightening sight to Parker's men. In their bright red waistcoats and carrying muskets and bayonets, the British redcoats, as they were called, seemed to outclass their opponents. The Minutemen were dressed in regular, probably worn-out clothes, and they carried old muskets.

Major John Pitcairn was leading the first British troops to arrive at Lexington Green. From his horse, he told the Minutemen to put down their muskets and leave. He shouted, "Throw down your arms! Ye villains, ye rebels." Captain Parker saw the danger in the situation and ordered his men to back away. The Minutemen followed their captain's command—but they did not do what Major Pitcairn had ordered. They held on to their weapons as they started to turn around.

Actors dressed as British redcoats march as if to battle.

Actors dressed as Minutemen

Suddenly a shot was fired. Some say it came from a redcoat's rifle. Others say that a Minuteman may have fired first. No matter how it started, that single shot

21

The Battle of Lexington turned to chaos as shots rang out between the Minutemen and British redcoats.

marked the beginning of the American Revolutionary War. The battle was soon under way.

Shots rang out from both sides and continued for several minutes. Major Pitcairn ordered his men to stop, but he was not heard. Finally, the British commander, Colonel Smith, arrived. He had a British drummer beat out a command to stop shooting, and the fighting ended. Only one British soldier was hurt, but eight Minutemen were dead and 10 were wounded.

The townspeople were shocked and shaken. As the colonists rushed to help their wounded men, the British fired a victory salute and marched on toward Concord. One can imagine the strong desire for revenge the Minutemen felt as they watched the British march away.

A week after the Battle of Lexington, American Captain John Parker wrote this description of what happened.

THE BATTLE OF CONCORD

Meanwhile, news of the British advance had reached
Concord. Colonel James Barrett was in charge of the 250
Minutemen who had gathered there. Barrett knew that the

In this historical painting, hundreds of British redcoats march into the center of Concord.

24

Americans had met the British at Lexington, but the reports were confusing. He didn't know if anyone had been killed. He also wasn't sure how close the British were or how many of them were marching.

So he sent a portion of his men toward Lexington to see what was happening. Soon they met the approaching British soldiers. The Minutemen saw that they were far outnumbered. Thaddeus Blood, a 19-year-old Minuteman, later wrote: "The sun was rising and shined on [them], and they made a noble appearance in their red coats and glistening arms."

The Minutemen turned back to town to report what they had seen. So as the Minutemen withdrew and the British marched on, both forces were marching into Concord. The marching soldiers in both armies were accompanied by drummers and fife players. The musicians helped the soldiers keep up their pace and their spirits. The music was also meant as a way to impress one's enemies and make them scared.

Drummers and fife players accompanied Minutemen during marches.

For this reason, perhaps, the American drummers and fife players picked up on the tune the British were playing and imitated it. Even though they were outnumbered, the Minutemen wanted to show that they were not scared. As Amos Barrett, a Minuteman, later wrote, "We had grand musick."

26

For the next few hours, the British and American soldiers stayed away from one another. Colonel Barrett had moved his Minutemen to a hill overlooking Concord's North Bridge. He wanted to avoid fighting if possible, but he didn't want to fully retreat. Barrett wanted to stay close to the British movements in Concord. He and his men still needed to protect the supplies there.

The Minutemen gathered above Concord's North Bridge.

The British soldiers divided into groups. One group of about 100 gathered on the opposite side of North Bridge, not far from the hill where the Minutemen were gathered. The Minutemen and this group of redcoats stared across the bridge at each other in silence. The

Minutemen from neighboring towns continued to march toward Concord throughout April 19, 1775.

alarmed British soldiers watched as more Minutemen and groups of colonial militia arrived from neighboring towns. The patriot forces were growing.

Meanwhile, other British soldiers were searching for the colonists' weapons. They found little, though, since the supplies had been moved from their original locations. At one point, the British set fire to some of the weapons they had found. Though it was only meant to destroy the weapons, the fire in the town's center was alarming. To the colonists, it appeared that the redcoats were going to destroy Concord.

The Minutemen leaders held a quick meeting. They all agreed to "march into the middle of town to defend their homes, or die in the attempt." Colonel Barrett ordered the men "not to fire till they [the British] fired first, then to fire as fast as we could." Captain Isaac Davis, one of the leaders, volunteered to lead the march. Davis was a popular captain, and his men followed him with pride.

*Captain Isaac Davis was the first Minuteman
to be killed at the Battle of Concord.*

It was an unusually warm spring day. As the Americans advanced toward the bridge, they passed by their farms where crops of grain were already sprouting. One soldier, David Brown, passed right by his own house, which the redcoats had earlier come to search.

There were 400 Minutemen marching now, and they far outnumbered the group of redcoats on the other side of the bridge. As the Americans drew near, the British took aim. British troops fired a few warning shots and then began shooting to kill. A fife player was wounded, and Captain Davis was killed.

Major John Buttrick, one of the Minutemen leaders, jumped up. "Fire, fellow soldiers, for God's sake, fire!" And fire they did. Musket balls whistled as they shot over the

30

bridge, and the smell of smoking gunpowder hung in the air. As the Americans pressed on, the British began to panic. British troops turned and ran back to town.

During the brief fight, three British and two American soldiers were killed. An important change had taken place—the colonial forces discovered that they could beat the mighty British!

Minutemen fire at the British across Concord's North Bridge.

RETREAT TO BOSTON

The Minutemen may have been part-time soldiers, but they were well-trained and well-organized. They had a strong cause and plenty of courage. This bold determination surprised the British soldiers. After the battles at Lexington and Concord, Britain's Colonel Smith was uncertain about his next move. His orders had been to seize American weapon supplies, but he had found very little. He wasn't sure if he should stay and fight the Americans or not.

As Colonel Smith considered his options, news of the battles spread throughout Massachusetts. Soon more than 1,000 Minutemen and militia arrived, and by the end of the day their forces would grow to more than 3,500. The Americans were ready to face the British as needed. Meanwhile, at around noon, Smith decided to march back to Boston. He didn't realize what a difficult journey it would be.

32

The British retreat from Concord.

The British soldiers had been trained to fight in an orderly manner, in straight lines and firing all at once. The Minutemen had learned some of their fighting techniques from the Indians. Instead of taking the enemy head on, the Minutemen hid along the road as the British made their

33

Minutemen surprised the British with fierce attacks as the redcoats tried to return to Boston.

way back to Boston. They crouched in the woods, on hills, and behind trees and rocks. They surrounded the British between two lines. Then they surprised them with attacks. The British tried to fire back, but the Americans were too good at hiding.

On a hill outside of Lexington, Captain Parker and the Minutemen were, once again, watching and waiting for the British to arrive. This time, however, the

Minutemen knew just what they were going to do. The British soldiers, by now very tired and hungry, came into view, and Parker and his men fired down on them. Colonel Smith was hit in the leg, and a number of redcoats went down.

By the time the British arrived in Lexington, they were at the point of surrendering. The reinforcements that Colonel Smith had requested early in the

British soldiers fell at surprising rates.

day arrived just in time. British General Hugh Percy

brought almost 1,000 more men and came equipped

with cannons.

*On a hill outside of Lexington, Captain Parker and his men took revenge
on the British for the day's earlier battle.*

Percy ordered his troops to use cannons to
destroy homes and to shoot any American soldiers they
encountered. However, many of the homes that the British

found were empty, and there were no Minutemen in sight. The Americans were playing a sophisticated game of hide-and-seek—and this game was very frustrating for the British.

For several hours, the Minutemen continued to fire on the British soldiers, and more and more of the redcoats were wounded and killed. Meanwhile, General Gage waited in Boston, not realizing how much had changed in one day.

Daylight was nearly gone by the time the British reached Boston. They were exhausted—and shocked. Never did they dream that the colonists would put up such a fight. More than 250 British soldiers had been killed, wounded, or captured that day, while the number of American casualties was fewer than 100. Those numbers may seem low by today's standards, but they made a statement to the British government. On April 19, 1775, the American colonies made one thing very clear: They were ready and willing to fight for their freedom.

THE REVOLUTION CONTINUES

After the battles of Lexington and Concord, the Minutemen saw very little action in the American Revolution. Since they were organized by town, it was difficult to have a central leadership. As the war with Great Britain continued, the Minutemen were soon replaced by the Continental Army, under the command of General George Washington.

In the years to come, many lives

George Washington and members of the Continental Army salute the first flag of the United States of America.

39

A statue of a Minuteman stands at the Minute Man National Historical Park in Concord, Massachusetts.

were lost on both sides of the war. In 1776, American leaders signed the Declaration of Independence, stating their intentions to be a new, independent nation. In 1783, a peace treaty with Great Britain was finally signed.

Even though their service in American history was limited, the Minutemen were some of the nation's most organized and prepared part-time soldiers. Without their bravery, the American Revolution could have ended in a much different way. Thanks to their efforts, the colonies had the courage to fight, and that fight eventually led to the creation of the United States of America.

GLOSSARY

bayonets—weapons, once common in battle, that are posts or rifles with blades on the end

casualties—soldiers who are injured, killed, captured, or missing in battle

fife—a musical instrument that is similar to a flute

militia—professional soldiers who are not part of a regular army

muskets—guns with long barrels used before rifles were invented

patriots—American colonists who wanted their independence from Britain; *patriots* also refers to people who love their country

reinforcements—additional soldiers sent in to strengthen troops in battle

retreat—to back away from a dangerous situation

DID YOU KNOW?

- British General Thomas Gage may have been betrayed by his own American-born wife. Some feel her loyalties were with the colonies and that she gave secret information to the patriots.

- Minuteman Captain John Parker was 45 years old in 1775 and was the father of seven. He also was ill with tuberculosis, a deadly disease of the lungs. Other Minutemen had more military experience than he did, but he was chosen as a leader perhaps because of his good judgment and calm personality.

- Captain Isaac Davis, the first Minuteman to be killed at the Battle of Concord, had a feeling that he might die when he left home on April 19, 1775. A few days before, an owl had come into his home, perched on his gun, and didn't seem to want to leave. To Davis, this was a bad sign. His final words to his wife on that April morning were, "Take good care of the children."

- The kind of musket that both the British and the Minutemen used was called the Brown Bess. A Brown Bess weighed 10 pounds (4.5 kilograms) and had a long barrel about 3 feet 8 inches (1.1 meter) long. It made a thick cloud of smoke each time it was fired.

IMPORTANT DATES

Timeline

1770	Colonists and British soldiers fight one another in the Boston Massacre. Five Americans are killed.
1773	In Boston, patriots dump British tea into the harbor, an event that becomes known as the Boston Tea Party.
1774	General Thomas Gage, a British general appointed by King George III, becomes military governor of the Massachusetts colony.
1775	On April 18, Paul Revere warns the Minutemen that the British are headed to Concord. On April 19, Minutemen fight the British at the battles of Lexington and Concord.
1776	The Declaration of Independence is signed.
1781	Fighting between the American colonies and the British troops ends.
1783	The United States and Great Britain sign the Treaty of Paris, and the war is officially ended.

IMPORTANT PEOPLE

JAMES BARRETT (18th century)
Colonel who led the Minutemen at Concord

ISAAC DAVIS (1745–1775)
Minuteman who led a charge against the British at Concord's North Bridge and was killed in battle

THOMAS GAGE (1721–1787)
British general who served as military governor of Massachusetts

JOHN PARKER (1729–1775)
Captain who led the Minutemen at Lexington

JOHN PITCAIRN (1722–1775)
Major who led British troops at Lexington and Concord

PAUL REVERE (1734–1818)
Boston silversmith and messenger whose famous ride alerted the Minutemen to the British advance

FRANCIS SMITH (1720?–1791)
British lieutenant colonel who led troops at Lexington and Concord

WANT TO KNOW MORE?

At the Library

Anderson, Dale. *The American Revolution.* Austin, Tex.: Raintree Steck-
Vaughn, 2003.

McCarthy, Pat. *The Thirteen Colonies from Founding to Revolution in
American History.* Berkeley Heights, N.J.: Enslow, 2004.

Raatma, Lucia. *The Battles of Lexington & Concord.* Minneapolis: Compass
Point Books, 2004.

Ross, Stewart. *The American Revolution.* New York: Franklin Watts, 2001.

On the Web

For more information on the *Minutemen*, use FactHound to track down
Web sites related to this book.

1. Go to *www.facthound.com*

2. Type in a search word related to
this book or this book ID: 0756508428.

3. Click on the *Fetch It* button.

Your trusty FactHound will fetch the best Web sites for you!

On the Road

Concord Museum

200 Lexington Road

Concord, MA 01742

978/369-9763

To learn more about the history of
Concord, Massachusetts

**Minute Man
National Historical Park**

174 Liberty St.

Concord, MA 01742

978/369-6993

To visit the sites of the opening

battles of the American Revolution

Look for more We the People books about this era:

The Battles of Lexington & Concord

The Bill of Rights

The Boston Massacre

The Boston Tea Party

The Declaration of Independence

Great Women of the American Revolution

Monticello

Mount Vernon

Paul Revere's Ride

The Stamp Act of 1765

The U.S. Constitution

Valley Forge

A complete list of We the People titles is available on our Web site:
www.compasspointbooks.com

INDEX

About the Author

Lucia Raatma received her bachelor's degree in English literature from the University of South Carolina and her master's degree in cinema studies from New York University. She has written a wide range of books for young people. When she is not researching or writing, she enjoys going to movies, practicing yoga, and spending time with her family. She lives in New York.